AF483078

Locs Not Dreads

JASMINE LOUIS

Illustrated by: Garrett Myers

Locs Not Dreads

Produced by HOV Publishing,
a division of HOV, LLC.
Bridgeport, CT

Illustrator: Garrett Myers

ISBN: 979-8-218-54949-7 (hard case)

Printed in the United States of America

Dedication

"To all the beautiful women in my family with locs, thank you for teaching me to love my hair by always wearing yours proudly. I hope this book will uplift someone the way you have always done for me."

Naomi had big, curly hair.
She often wore it in styles with lots of flair.

But what Naomi didn't like
was how much it hurt to
get her hairdo just right.

She would sit in a chair and wail
while Mama yanked, tugged, and
pulled at her ponytail.

Oh, how Naomi loved how her hair looked,
but she couldn't handle all the pain the beauty took.

One day, Naomi sat down in the
chair and whined and cried.
Mama, who had enough, yelled,
"It's time! It's time!"

"We can lock your hair. It'll look brand new.
You can wear it however you'd like,
and it won't hurt to do."

Naomi thought for a second if she
should go through with this
because her afro was one she
would surely miss.

But she also thought about getting her hair done.
It hurt so bad!
If she didn't have to suffer through that again,
she'd be more than glad.

"Alright," she said. "As long as
it doesn't hurt one bit."
"Good," replied her mom.
"I'm glad you'll do it."

Mama booked an appointment
and took Naomi to the salon.
It was finally time to get her locs done.

She sat in the stylist's chair
and paid close attention as
the woman did her hair.

She waited for the pain, but it rarely came.
And when it did, it hadn't hurt the same.

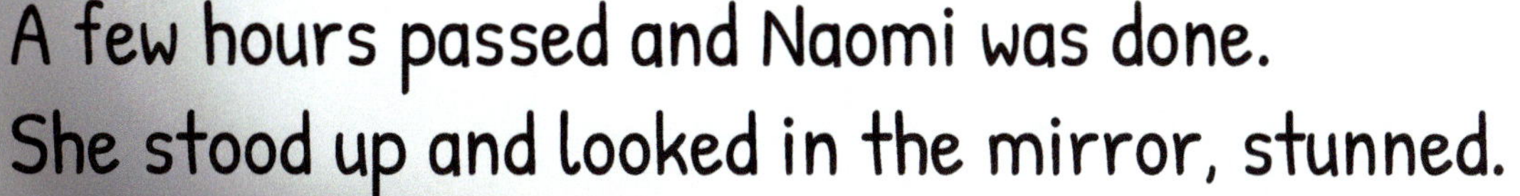

A few hours passed and Naomi was done.
She stood up and looked in the mirror, stunned.

"My hair is oh so chic! It's every bit of unique!"

She thanked the hairdresser and left with Mama.
They went home and ate some lasagna.

"I love my dreads," she told Mama and Pop.
Mama set her fork down, looking shocked.

"We don't use that word," Pop said.
"It was given by people who thought our
hair was full of dread."

"Why would anyone think that way?
I could rock this style every day."

Mama spoke, "We wear our hair proud,
don't let anyone try to put you down."

That's exactly what Naomi did as she walked into school.

She was a little fashionista with her locs looking cool.

The kids all turned to look at her.
"Are those dreads?" one of them asked, nose upturned.

"Locs not dreads," Naomi replied.
"I love my hair, and I wear it with pride!"

At lunch and as she walked around school,
she got a few compliments on her new 'do.
But the one thing she didn't appreciate
was what they called her hair, that word of hate.

"Locs not dreads," she would say with a sigh.
"I love my hair and I wear it with pride!"

On the playground as she played four-square,
everyone came to have a look at her hair.
They begged, "Can I touch your dreads? Pretty
please?"

"I'd rather you not," Naomi said with ease.

"And they're locs not dreads," she added to her reply. "I love my hair and I wear it with pride!"

When school was done,
Mama and Pop picked her up
and asked about her day,
which was filled with fun.

"I did exactly what you said.
Now everybody knows not to
call my locs dreads."

She got home and went to her
room to do her work,
but on her way to her desk,
something caught her eye and she jerked.

Naomi looked in the mirror at the
locs swinging down her back.
Her locs were cute. She knew that!

"Locs not dreads," Naomi said
with a smile she couldn't hide.
"I love my hair. I wear it with pride."

THE END!

About the Author

Jasmine Louis is the award-winning poet and author of *A Christmas Mouse* and *My World View Through Poetry*. Born and raised in Virginia, Jasmine lives with her parents and triplet siblings. She is currently attending her first year of college at the age of 16.

Jasmine's passion for writing began at a young age, and she published her first book at nine years old. Since then, she's been recognized numerous times for her talent. When she's not writing, Jasmine can be found on the track, crocheting on the couch, or spending time with her three dogs, Cross, Tux, and Caesar.